OLD DOG, NEW TRICKS

Also by Dick Cate

FLYING FREE
A FUNNY SORT OF CHRISTMAS
(Antelopes)

OLD DOG, NEW TRICKS

Dick Cate

Illustrated by
Trevor Stubley

HAMISH HAMILTON
LONDON

First published in Great Britain 1978
by Hamish Hamilton Children's Books, Limited,
90 Great Russell Street, London WC1B 3PT

ISBN 0 241 89949 4

Printed photolitho in Great Britain by
Ebenezer Baylis and Son Ltd
The Trinity Press, Worcester, and London

To Cathy

Contents

CHAPTER ONE

Grandma in Trouble

BILLY'S GRANDMA WAS in trouble again. She had gone to Durham market for some vegetables and come back with a dog instead.

"I honestly think you're barmy, Mother," Billy's mam said to her. "However do you think you're going to look after a dog at your age?"

"I haven't got one foot in the grave yet, Our Alice," grandma said. "I'm not so old as I can't manage a dog!"

As far as Billy was concerned, he was glad they had a dog in the family again. It made things seem complete somehow. It was ages since his dad had said they might be getting another one—so long ago that Billy had begun to give up hope.

Mind you, the dog that grandma had

brought back was not exactly a beauty. Steven—who was married to Billy's sister—said it would win first prize in any Ugly Competition. And he wasn't far off the mark. Even grandma called it a liquorice allsort to its face. That was because it appeared to have so many different sorts of breed in it.

Neither was it what you might call sensible. It was as daft as a brush, dashing about from pillar to post, knocking things over, and jumping up on your lap. Steven kept saying it had ants in its pants.

Grandma had got it from the R.S.P.C.A. man in the market. He had told her that lots of people were buying dogs for pets and then losing interest in them in no time. They turned them loose in the streets.

"It's a crying shame!" grandma had said. "What happens to them after that?"

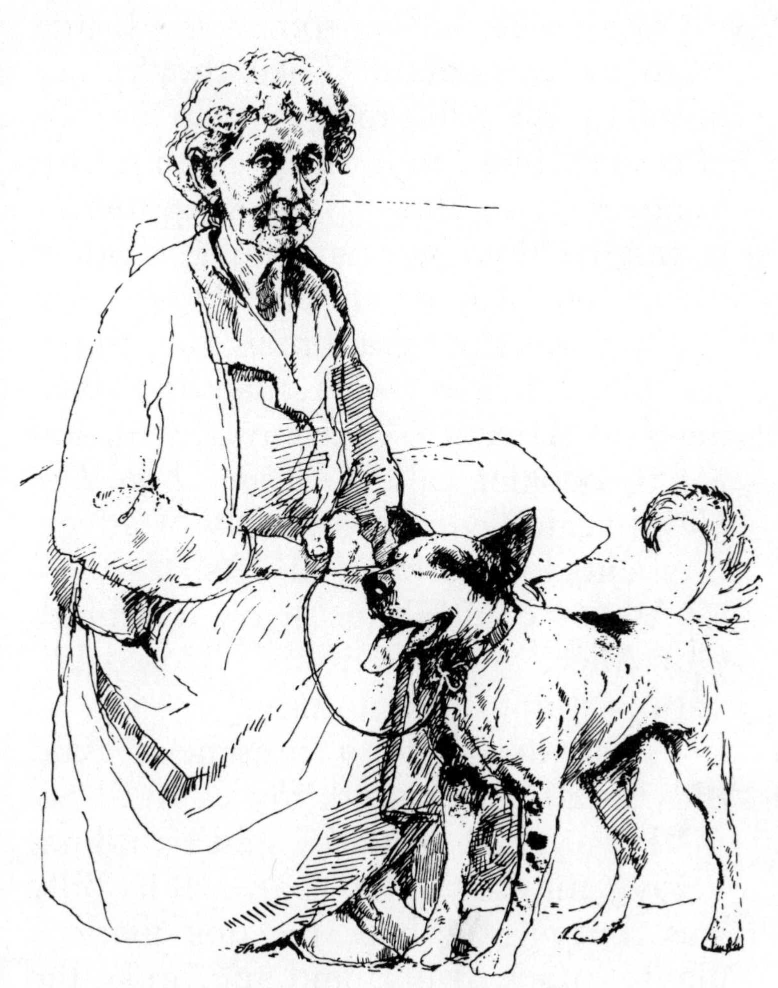

"If they're lucky, somebody brings them to us, madam. Then they're our problem. We'd like to keep them forever, of course. But I'm afraid we can't. Our finances won't allow it. We keep them a fortnight, then we have to get rid of them—one way or another."

That was how grandma came to get the dog. The R.S.P.C.A. man had given her a bit of string to lead it away with and a free booklet called *Keeping Your Dog Happy* which consisted mostly of advertisements for worming tablets.

"Well I couldn't just leave it behind, Our Alice," said grandma. "Could I?"

Billy's mam said nothing.

"That dog'll be a nuisance," said Billy's dad. "Just mark my words."

"It's as good as gold," said grandma.

Five minutes after that, while Billy was romping with it, the dog made a playful snack at his hand and broke the skin.

Grandma washed the finger with T.C.P. and put a bandage on it. Billy liked that. Having a bandaged-up finger made him feel a bit like a wounded soldier. A bit of a hero.

Later, on their way home, they called in at Steve and Sandra's house, and Billy was proud to show them his wounded finger.

"You want to be careful with that, kiddar," said Steve.

"What for, Steve?"

"Whatever you do, don't let the doctor see it," said Steve. "Doctors are always on the look-out for spare finger ends. Isn't that right, Sandra?"

"Rubbish!" said Sandra, who was busy washing the baby, Alice Margaret Julie.

Billy pretended to believe him.

"What do they want spare finger ends for, Steve?" he asked.

"They want them for people that have lost them in accidents down the pit," said Steve.

"For goodness sake give over, Steve!" said Sandra. "What a horrible thing to say!"

Billy tried to look as if he half-believed Steve, but inside he was just laughing to himself. He went over to Sandra and started to make goo-goo noises at Alice Margaret Julie. She gurgled back at him

and rocked back and forth with delight as Sandra supported her.

"She really knows Our Billy!" said Sandra.

"Doesn't she, though!" said Billy's mother. "Just look at her little eyes! There's real intelligence for you!"

Billy pushed his face closer and made his goo-goo noise again. Alice Margaret Julie laughed and squealed. She kicked and jerked so much that Sandra had a job holding on to her soapy little body.

They were all ringed round her, laughing, full of approval.

All of them except Billy's dad, that is.

He was standing by the window with his back to them.

Sandra glanced over at him, then back at her mum. "What's up with me dad?" she asked quietly. "Is it the news?"

Billy's mother nodded. "He's a bit depressed, Our Sandra," she said. "He's taken it badly."

Billy wondered what news they were talking about. Whatever it was, *he* hadn't heard it yet.

"There's nowt certain yet," said Steve. "Nowt to worry about."

"No," said Billy's mam, as though she didn't quite believe him.

Minutes later, when they were out in the street again and his dad was a few steps ahead of them as usual, Billy asked his mam what news they had been talking about.

She didn't even look at him.

All she said was: "Be quiet, Our Billy."

That was all.

She didn't speak another word.

Grandma kept the dog for exactly a week.

By that time it had chewed a hole in a clippy-mat, broken an ornament (a present from Blackpool: not really very valuable, but treasured all the same), and nearly frightened the life out of an old man with a walking stick who just happened to pass grandma's front gate.

"What a week this has been, Alice," gran said. "I don't want another week like this one—not as long as I live!"

They were all sitting in the kitchen where it was cooler. They had the back door wide open. They were enjoying a nice cup of tea, and Billy was wondering if he'd sat there long enough to be allowed to go into the front room and watch the telly.

When all of a sudden there was this horrible noise.

What had happened was that the dog had got hold of the cat next door. The pair of them were snarling and scratching all over grandma's seedling beds.

Billy's dad had hold of the dog in no time. He whirled it up into the air. It still held on to the cat. Then Billy's dad hit

the dog one sharp tap on the end of its nose. The dog yelped. The cat fell twisting to the ground. In half a second it was over the fence and out of sight. Billy's dad began to untangle the pieces of thread and milk bottle tops that were wrapped around the dog's legs. That was grandma's invention for keeping the birds away.

For grandma, this was the last straw as far as keeping the dog was concerned.

"Them seeds was just doing nicely, Our Alice," she said. "And I *can't* have it going after the next-door cat. They *worship* that cat next door. *Worship* it. I couldn't bear anything to happen to it. It's a nice little cat. It used to come to me for scraps. I'm sorry, but the dog will just have to go. I've tried my best with it, but I just can't manage!"

Nobody spoke for a long time.

Billy realized that the telly was out of the question just now. It was always like this when there was something good on like *It's a Knockout*!

Then Billy's dad looked across at his mother.

"What do *you* think?" he said.

"*I* don't want the dog—if that's what you're asking me," said Billy's mother. "I've got enough on my plate, thank you!"

"It only wants training up," said grandma.

"You've been very silly, Mother!" said Billy's mam. "I knew it would come to this. You should never have got the dog in the first place."

"It's no good crying over spilt milk," said Billy's dad.

"I'll help to train it, Mam," said Billy, quickly.

"You shut up!" she said.

There was another pause.

"Well?" said Billy's dad. "Shall we give it a try?"

"*I* don't want the dog," said Billy's mam.

"I don't want it either if it comes to that!" said Billy's dad. "Especially just now. But that's not the point, is it? The point is—do you want the dog to be put down or not?"

"No."

"Well, then," said Billy's dad, "that's that! We shall just have to take it, want it or not."

CHAPTER TWO

Bad News

ONE NIGHT BILLY came home for his tea and saw his dad sitting by the fire, staring into the flames.

"How do, Dad," said Billy.

His dad didn't reply.

Billy went through into the back-kitchen.

His mother was using the new-fangled potato peeler they'd bought at Bishop Auckland market. The man who had demonstrated it had made it look easy as wink to use: but when Billy's mam had first tried it she had nearly lost her thumb.

That was a fortnight ago. Billy could see that his mother was improving with the new peeler. It was true that her peelings were still twice as thick as the market man's had been: but at least they weren't as thick as elephants' toenails any more.

"Mam?"

"What is it, Billy?"

"What's up with me dad?"

"There's nothing up with your dad."

"Is he in a bad temper or something?"

"Don't be daft, Our Billy. And stop dabbling your fingers in my tatie water—it's mucky enough already, isn't it!"

"Is it something to do with the dog?"

"Course it isn't!"

"Where is the dog, anyhow?"

"Out in the back-yard. Your dad said it was getting under his feet."

Through the window Billy could just see the dog lying in the shade of the coal-house, looking miserable as sin. It was panting hard, its tongue lolling out.

"Has it got any water, Mam?"

His mother gave him a sharp look.

"Do you think I'd leave a dog out on a hot day like this without a drink of water, Billy?"

"I can't see it," said Billy.

"That's because I put it in the shade, behind the tin bath."

The dog had heard their voices and was looking towards the window, hope-

fully. It couldn't see them because of the net curtains.

Billy felt sorry for it. It was typical, he

thought, that they hadn't bought a proper lead for it yet. They had had it for a month now, and still just used a piece of string to take it out for walks or tie it up.

Billy was worried about it as well. It was always doing something wrong. The other night it had jumped onto Sandra's knee without being asked and ruined her tights.

All it wanted, of course, was a bit of attention. But the trouble was nobody loved the dog. His dad scarcely noticed it. His mother fed it, but that was about all. The trouble was it was so clumsy and stupid. When Billy took it for walks it kept belting off without taking any notice of him. Even Billy felt angry with it then.

His mother finished the potatoes now. She washed the peeler under the tap and wiped it clean.

"Do you like the new peeler now, Mam?"

"It's all right," she said. "It's just a

matter of getting used to it, that's all."

"Mam?"

"What is it now, Billy?"

She had just picked up the oven-glove and was about to open the oven-door. She didn't want to be interrupted.

"There is something up with me dad, isn't there?"

She took a swift breath of annoyance. But then the look on her face softened.

She bent down to him and whispered quietly:

"They're going to close down the pit, Our Billy. It's definite now. Your dad will lose his job."

CHAPTER THREE

Billy Loses His Trifle

It wasn't just that they were closing down the pit. They were going to dismantle the pit-head. They were going to smash down the engine-house and the lamp-cabin and the baths and the changing rooms. When Billy tried to imagine these things, he just couldn't. It seemed impossible.

His dad pretended to laugh about it all: but his laughter was bitter and hollow, as though he didn't believe in it himself.

Steven, though, wasn't a bit worried. The following Sunday evening, for instance, when they were all having supper at Billy's house, he was joking about it.

He reckoned that when the pit closed the council had plans to turn the village into a holiday resort for people who found Spain too hot and sunny.

"It's all right laughing, Steven," said Billy's mam as she served out the bubble and squeak, "but what sort of job will you get when the pit's closed?"

Billy was just piling two cushions on top of the pouffe because they were one chair short.

"Any sort of job that's going," said Steve. "I've got two hands, haven't I? And I'm not as daft as I look."

"You couldn't be as daft as you look," said Sandra, who was noted for her sharp tongue.

"Getting a job round here is going to be easier said than done," said Billy's dad.

"Then we'll shift," said Steve. "Down in Yorkshire they're crying out for able-bodied men."

"No use you applying, then!" said Sandra.

HP

But nobody laughed.

"But how will you get on with the people down there?" asked Billy's mam.

"They're still human beings down in Yorkshire, you know, Mother-in-law. I mean, they haven't got three legs and bananas growing out of their ears."

"I've heard tell that Yorkshiremen are tight-fisted," said Billy's dad. "They say they're worse than Scotsmen."

"Eye-wash!" said Steve. "I never met a mingy Scotsman yet!"

"Well, I think moving is a good idea," said grandma. Up to now she'd been concentrating on her supper. "A change is as good as a rest, I say. And the best time to move is when you're young and fit. I only wish somebody would give me the chance to move to Yorkshire. I'd go like a shot."

"Don't be silly, Mother," said Billy's mam, "It's time for you to put your feet up."

"I'll put my feet up when I'm dead, Alice, and not before!" said grandma.

"Tell you what, Grandma," said Steve. "We'll buy you a push-bike before we go and then you can bike it down there and help us with the decorating one weekend!"

"I might just do that and all," said grandma. "It'll not be the first time I've been on a push-bike, and there's life in the old horse yet!"

They laughed so much that they didn't hear the knock at the front door.

It was Mr Murray, their new neighbour. Billy's man and dad weren't over keen on the Murrays. They were forever borrowing things: sugar, matches, bits of string. Twice they had asked to borrow a poker—of all things! ("Haven't they got a poker of their own, for goodness' sake!" Billy's mam had said.)

But if *they* didn't hear the knock at the door, the dog did.

So far that night it had been on its best behaviour: all it had done was tangle up some wool and eat a clothes-peg.

But when it heard the knock it went straight for the door and just happened to knock over Billy's pouffe.

Billy went over backwards, his knees

hit the table, his trifle (which he'd been looking forward to all night) went up in the air—and landed upside-down on his chest.

"That dog's a menace, Alice!" said

grandma. "Somebody wants to train it up!"

"Well, Mother!" said Billy's mam, absolutely flabbergasted.

"It's true what I tell you," said grandma. "Nobody looks after it properly!"

CHAPTER FOUR

The Pit Heap

GRANDMA WAS RIGHT. They *didn't* look after the dog properly. They fed it, of course. They saw that it always had water. But nobody really bothered with it.

In an attempt to put that matter right Billy borrowed a book from the mobile library called *Dog Training for Beginners*.

The first chapter told you that to get the dog to come to your word of command you had to say "Here!" or "Heel!" every time.

But every time Billy said "Here!" or "Heel!" the dog ran off in the opposite direction: it was full of enthusiasm, but it just didn't seem to understand.

Billy began to think Steve might be right when he said it had a peabrain.

One evening he went for a walk with Steve and Sandra in the field next to the colliery. Alice Margaret Julie was with them, in her pram.

The dog was barking wildly, chasing after sticks which Steve was throwing for it. Steve wanted it to bring the sticks back, but it didn't seem to get the idea. It kept dropping them. Or it would go racing after some white doves which kept alighting on the path ahead of them to waddle along for a yard or two like important busybodies. But at least the dog was amusing everybody. They were all having a good laugh at its antics. That was something.

They needed a good laugh nowadays. Especially at Billy's house. His dad was getting more and more miserable every day. It was quite certain now that the pit was closing down.

Steve had got a job in a pit near Barnsley.

"At any rate, they've got a football team, kiddar," he had said to Billy.

"Barnsley, you mean? They're hopeless!"

"Don't forget they won the cup once, kiddar."

"Did they? When?"

"Nineteen hundred and twelve."

"Blimey! That was yonks ago."

"That makes no odds, kiddar. It shows they were great once. And if they were great once they can be great again. Just wait till *I* get down there and start cheering them on. They'll have the cup back in no time."

"You can say that again," said Sandra. "With a mouth like yours cheering them on they can't fail!"

Billy's dad had been there at the time. But he hadn't smiled or laughed. He sat there for ages nowadays, not saying a word to anybody. Sometimes he took his mouth-organ and sat on the stairs in the dark and played tunes to himself.

The trouble was, he didn't want to leave his home, but he didn't want to learn another job either.

"I'm too old to learn new ways," he kept saying. "I'm a collier. All I can do is dig coal."

"That's daft talk," Billy's mother replied. "If you want to stop here you'll

just *have* to learn another job. And that's that!"

"Talk sense, woman!" he would say angrily. "Talk sense!"

Billy thought of his dad now. The field they were walking in had once been used for pit ponies. In the old days they had been used to pull the tubs of coal from the coal-face to the pit-shaft bottom. They had been stabled underground, only now and then being brought up out of the darkness of the pits. Some of them had gone blind through being kept down there too long. But the miners had loved them, all the same. They had looked after them well, given them nicknames, saved titbits of cheese and apple and bread for them. So that although the pit ponies had been hard-worked, at the same time they had in many ways been treated as pets. And when they had come up into the fields, either for a rest or to retire, they had been treated like proper little champions.

They were all gone now, of course. Nowadays the coal was carried to the pit-shaft by conveyor belt.

But if the ponies had long since gone the pit heap still remained. It towered over the field. It had taken almost seventy years to grow to this size, covering first one field, then another, then a small wood, then more fields. It had filled in streams and buried hedges.

Billy had climbed to the top of it once. Up the ravines and gullies that the wind and rain had carved on its surface. He had been quite puffed out when he reached the summit. Far below him the streets of the village across the valley had looked small and unimportant. The people walking up and down them had looked like insects.

Now, they were going to level the heap. They were going to put soil on it. Make grass grow. Stick cows and sheep on it.

Billy looked up at the pit heap. It was big and black and ugly. But he knew he'd feel sorry when it had gone, when it had been reduced to a pale memory.

"I'm just going over to the heap, Our Sandra," he called.

"Mind you don't get mucky, then. Remember you've got your best shoes on!"

He knew they wouldn't want to come with him. They wouldn't want to spoil their new pram banging it over the field. Besides, Sandra wouldn't let Alice Margaret Julie anywhere near The Stinky Beck that ran along the bottom of the heap. It ponged like anything. And there were rats in it.

Billy was thinking that this might be the last time he crossed the colliery field. The other night his dad had said they might have to leave after all. There were no jobs in the area. "And we have to work to live, Billy," he had said. "It's as simple as that."

It seemed to Billy that he knew every tussock of grass in this field. The trees that stood round it seemed like old friends. He knew where there were five nests down at the other end where the hawthorns were as plump and comfy as tea-cosies. And up in the far corner he knew a marshy bit where you could get tadpoles every year.

In a way, these things seemed to *belong*

to him. Or perhaps that wasn't it. Perhaps it was that *he* belonged to them. Or was it that they belonged to one another?

He ducked under the rusty wire of the fence. He walked along the bank of The Stinky Beck until he reached the railway sleeper that acted as a footbridge. Who had put that sleeper there? It had been there ever since he could remember. And why had it been put there anyhow? Was it

just so that he and other boys could walk over it? Was that the reason?

Once over the beck he walked a step or two up the side of the heap. He scuffed at the coarse grey waste in his new shoes. Dry, hard stuff it was. The weeds that managed to survive on it looked yellow and limp.

Down by The Stinky Beck the reeds and coltsfoot flourished, though. There was always plenty of water down in the pit The Stinky Beck came from. Sometimes Billy's dad worked in two or three feet of water. It had probably been down there in the bowels of the earth for hundreds of years, waiting to be pumped out and flow under the sun again.

As he watched, a water-rat plumped into the water and began to swim across. Normally Billy didn't like rats, not even water-rats. They gave him the heeby-jeebies. Sometimes rats got into their hen-hut and pinched the eggs. People said that

rats were so sly that one would clutch an egg to its tummy and lie on its back while another dragged it away by the tail.

Billy watched its nose forming a spreading vee as it pushed through the grey water. When it reached the other side it heaved itself onto a stone.

Rats never hurried, Billy had noticed. They always took their time. It was the slowness of rats that frightened you. Their slowness and bigness.

The water-rat seemed to be looking at Billy. It didn't seem too worried. It began to clean its whiskers.

Billy didn't want to frighten it away. It occurred to him that this might be the last time he would ever see a water-rat in The Stinky Beck. So he sat very still, not moving a muscle.

CHAPTER FIVE

Mr Murray Calls

WHEN THE PIT closed, Billy's dad was thrown out of work. He had to go to the Social Security office to get his money. The people who worked there treated him in a snooty manner. They made him feel ashamed.

He was offered another job in the pits. But that was down in Yorkshire, near Barnsley, where Steve and Sandra had moved. But he didn't want to do that, not just yet.

"We'll hang on here for a bit longer. See if something turns up. My roots are in this place now. I'm too old to shift," he said one night.

"And what do you think's going to turn up in this place?" Billy's mam said. She was getting the dirty clothes ready to take down to the launderette. "There's nothing in this place! Nothing at all!"

Then she went out, banging the door behind her.

Billy's dad was always getting on her nerves nowadays. Now that he had no proper work of his own, he kept wanting to do her jobs instead. He was always drying the dishes and putting them away in the wrong place or beating the mats in the back-yard when she had washing hanging up on the line.

"I just wish your dad would get himself out somewhere," she once said to Billy. "Anywhere—just so long as he gets out from under my feet. I wish he'd go for a walk, or something."

He *did* go out for walks. Sometimes he took the dog with him. But not often. He had no time for the dog, really. He hardly ever noticed her.

And that was a pity. Because the dog seemed to like Billy's dad more than she

Echo

liked all the rest of them. She made a real fuss of him when he came back into the house (usually knocking something over with her tail). And when he was sitting in his chair just staring at the fire she used to sit beside him and push her nose into his hand as though trying to cheer him up. Not that it did any good.

The one thing that did cheer up Billy's dad was the letters they got from Sandra. They were mostly about Alice Margaret Julie, about nine-tenths of every letter as far as Billy could make out. But she also told them about the Tupperware Club she went to, and the cheapness of clothes in Barnsley market, and what colour they were going to decorate the bathroom (oyster pink!), and the weather (which was more or less the same as it was where Billy lived—baking hot), and all about the curtains they'd got from the Co-op for only forty pence a yard.

"Fancy that!" Billy's mother had said.

"Forty pence a yard! You can't get curtains that cheap up here!"

And she couldn't get over the fact that Sandra and Steve had a semi-detached house now. It was what she had always fancied herself. Or so she said.

"What for?" Billy's dad would ask her. It always narked him. "What's the matter with a terrace house?"

Billy could see that it was nice in some ways, living in a terrace. You had two sets of neighbours instead of one. It made you feel comfy, and close to other people. You only had to bang on your fire-back with a poker and your neighbours would be round in a tick to see what you wanted. The trouble was that just at the moment they didn't have a poker at Billy's house. The Murrays had borrowed it again.

"I wonder what they keep wanting the poker for, Dad?" Billy asked one day.

"I often wonder meself, Billy," he said. "It's a proper mystery."

One night towards the end of August Mr Murray came round to their house.

"That'll be him next door," said Billy's mother. "I wonder what he wants to borrow this time?"

But he'd come to tell them about a job at the factory where he worked.

He was a young man with broad shoulders. He was always in his boiler suit (Billy's mother said he must sleep in it!) and he seemed to wear nothing underneath it because you could see all the hairs on his chest.

"What sort of job is it, Mr Murray?" asked Billy's mam. Face to face she always called him Mr Murray, but when he wasn't there she referred to him as 'him next door.' They never called him Frank—which he kept asking them to.

"It's a driving job," he said. "Driving a little van. The chap who does it now is leaving next month."

"That sounds interesting," she said.

She was clearing the things from the table and wiping up the breadcrumbs. She liked the house to be clean and tidy, especially when they had a visitor.

"The only trouble is, I can't drive," said Billy's dad.

"You can always learn."

"Don't talk soft, woman. I'm too old to learn new tricks. I'm like that dog."

And when he said that, the dog pricked up her ears and looked at him. Billy was surprised and pleased. It showed the dog had *some* sense.

"Only I happen to know they're on the look-out for somebody with a bit of maturity, like," said Mr Murray. "The two drivers they had before were young lads—they both had a lot of accidents. The last one cost the firm three hundred pounds in repairs in two weeks."

That made Billy's dad look up with a bit of interest.

"I'll give it a bit of thought," he said.

"You do that," said Mr Murray. "And if you want to learn to drive just let me know. I'll be glad to show you how."

There was another awkward pause.

"That's very kind of you, I'm sure," said Billy's mam. "Well, Mr Murray, I'll just show you to the door."

"I wish you'd call me Frank," he said. "Oh, by the way—I nearly forgot—you haven't got such a thing as a bit of sugar you could spare?"

Billy nearly burst out laughing. He had to hold his sides while his mother went into the kitchen and came back with some sugar in a bag.

As soon as Mr Murray had gone he let the laughter out.

"It's not a laughing matter, Billy!" his mother said sharply.

Then she looked at his father.

"Well?" she said.

"Well what?"

"Are you going to try for that job or not?"

"I'll never learn to drive, woman," he said, "not in a month of Sundays."

CHAPTER SIX

The First Real Smile in Weeks

IN FACT, BILLY's dad learnt to drive in just under a month. This was largely due to the fact that Mr Murray took him out every night and gave him a driving lesson.

They discovered that Mr Murray was a fanatic on cars. He had a barn down at the end of the village and he collected old cars (especially Rovers) and took bits and pieces off them and built up one good car out of three useless ones.

They also found out why Mr Murray kept borrowing their poker. The Rover manufacturers didn't make the right sort of rubber piping for the old cars any more, not exactly the right size. But Mr Murray had found that by heating Billy's dad's poker and pushing it into the bore of the

new rubber pipes, it made the hole just right.

So that was one mystery explained.

Most nights Billy went out with them on their practice runs. It amused Billy to see his dad learning to drive. He kept doing things wrong the way Billy did at school when they had sums.

And sometimes he got told off.

"That's no good!" Mr Murray would say. "That's not what I told you to do! Lift your foot off the clutch gently!"

"I don't know," Billy's dad would say, shaking his head. "I'm a proper duffer at this game, Frank."

They all called him Frank now.

And Billy's dad gave him the poker to keep. He got a pal of his who used to be the colliery blacksmith to make a new one for them.

Billy's dad had lots of pals.

One of them happened to be the examiner who took him for his driving test. They had been down the pit together for six years before the other man had to leave because of dust on the lungs.

"Well look who it is!" said the examiner as soon as he saw Billy's dad at the test centre. "If it isn't my old pal, Dick!"

Up till then Billy's dad had been shaking like a leaf. But after that he wasn't nervous at all.

"I don't think I'd have passed, not if it had been another examiner," he said. "I made a couple of mistakes, you know."

"Don't be daft!" said Billy's mother with a laugh. "Everybody makes mistakes. They're bound to."

"Aye, I suppose they are," said Billy's dad.

And for the first time in weeks he gave a real smile.

CHAPTER SEVEN

Barnsley, here we come!

BILLY'S DAD WAS allowed to use the firm's van at weekends and they drove down to see Steve and Sandra and the baby as soon as Billy's dad thought he was safe enough to carry passengers.

By then the hot weather had gone. One minute the Water Board men were scampering around putting up stand-pipes at every corner, and the next minute the heavens opened and it rained, and rained, and rained.

"If it rains much longer we'll have to build another ark!" grandma said. Then, after a minute, she added: "Come to think of it, I wouldn't mind at all going on a sea voyage."

The rain was still pelting down as they joined the motorway.

"When *is* this rain going to stop?" asked Billy's mam.

She was trying to wipe all the steam from the inside of the windscreen with a wash-leather made of little bits.

Billy's dad didn't answer.

His eyes were almost popping out of his head with concentration. He was driving so slowly that two cars had overtaken them while they were still on the slip road. One of the drivers had honked at them and stared as he swept past. Billy's mother had stared back at him and shaken her fist. "Road-hog!" she had muttered.

Billy and his grandma were in the back of the van with Dot. That was what they called the dog now. They'd decided to call her that simply because she was the dottiest dog they'd ever had. They'd hummed and hawed about taking her at all, but eventually they'd taken her because if they had left her behind she might have eaten part of the sofa or bitten a leg off the best table.

Billy's mam had volunteered to travel in the back of the van, but grandma wouldn't hear of that.

"*I*'ll travel in the back, Our Alice," she said. "I hate them safety-belt things, and, besides, I can stretch my legs out in the back. We'll take the Monopoly, and me and Our Billy can play."

It seemed a good idea.

The trouble was that Dot kept standing on the board and eating the banknotes.

And just as they crossed the border into Yorkshire she did something even worse.

Billy and his grandma craned their necks to look out of the windscreen to see the sign with the white rose of Yorkshire on it. It was quite exciting seeing that—like entering a foreign country.

But when they turned back to the game, both the dice had gone: and Dot was chewing something.

"Blimey!" shouted Billy. "That blinking dog has got the dice!"

"Billy! I've told you not to swear!" shouted his mother, swivelling round in her seat.

100
GO

"That's not swearing, Our Alice," said grandma.

"DROP IT! DROP IT!" Billy was shouting.

Dot looked at him sweetly.

Then she swallowed.

"STUPID NIT!" shouted Billy.

"BILLY!" screamed his mother. "WATCH YOUR LANGUAGE!"

"SHUT UP, EVERYBODY!" yelled Billy's dad. "I'M TRYING TO DRIVE THIS VAN—IF YOU DON'T MIND!"

Everybody fell quiet then.

"Take you long to get down here?" called Steve from the kitchen where he was making a pot of tea.

"No time at all," said Billy's dad who was sitting by the lounge fire, his legs stretched out, puffing his pipe, looked pleased with himself.

"Easy journey?"

"Lovely," said Billy's dad. "Nothing to it."

Billy looked at his dad. Everybody had sat like mummies without speaking for twenty minutes after he had bawled at them. Even Dot had behaved herself. She had curled up on her blanket and gone to sleep. She always did that when she felt guilty.

Steve brought the tray in with the tea-pot and things on it. He placed it on the

coffee table he'd made last Christmas in their old home.

"How are things down here, then?" asked Billy's dad.

"Couldn't be better."

"You get on all right with the locals?"

"Champion, man. There's a bonny lot of folks here from Durham, you know."

"Is that a fact?"

"The feller next door is from Sunderland."

"Fancy that! It's a small world!"

Sandra had taken grandma and Billy's mother on a tour of the upstairs rooms. Billy could hear them clumping about above him. His mother kept saying, "Isn't that just lovely!" every few seconds. As they came back down the stairs into the lounge she said, "And I think you've got that bathroom really nice. It's like a picture, Our Sandra."

"Like a palace," said grandma.

"You want to go up and have a look at

that bathroom," Billy's mam said to his dad. "Them pink curtains is lovely."

"I will in a minute," said Billy's dad.

Steve was handing the tea round.

"Thanks. I'm dropping for a cup of tea," said Billy's mam.

She took a sip.

"Lovely. I always say there's nothing like a cup of tea."

She watched Steve hand a cup to Sandra who had just put Alice Margaret Julie down on the carpet.

"That's something *my* husband never does," she said.

"What's that?" asked Steve.

"Make a cup of tea," she said. "He'd no more think of it than fly!"

"Don't be daft," said Billy's dad. "What about that time ten years ago, when you were bad in bed with the 'flu? I made you a cup then."

They all laughed at that.

When Alice Margaret Julie started to

crawl again Billy's mother said for the tenth time: "Well, I've never in my life before seen a baby crawl that early!"

"She's forward for her age," said grandma. "There'll be no holding her once she gets going."

"There's no holding her now," said Billy's mam.

"She's fairly sprouting up," said grandma.

"Like a cabbage!" laughed Steve.

It rained all the afternoon. But that didn't stop them enjoying themselves. They talked so much that Steve almost missed the sports results.

"All my life, if there's one thing I've wanted, it's been a french window like yours, Our Sandra," said Billy's mam. "It must be lovely to walk straight out into your garden."

"If *we* had a french window, we'd walk straight out into the back-yard!" said Billy's dad.

And everybody laughed again—except Billy's mam.

There was only one unfortunate incident.

It happened when Sandra opened the french windows to show her mother exactly how they worked.

Dot rushed out into the garden. It took

them ten minutes to wipe up the muddy paw marks when she agreed to come back in.

"I'm terribly sorry, Our Sandra," said Billy's mam.

"It wants training, that dog!" said grandma.

"They'll wipe off with a cloth," said Sandra.

And even as she spoke Steve came back in from the kitchen with a damp sponge.

"Mind, Sandra," laughed grandma, "you've got *him* trained all right!"

When it was time for them to go Sandra asked them if they wouldn't rather stay the night.

"We have two spare rooms," said Steve.

"No, we won't overstay our welcome," said Billy's mam.

"What about you, Gran?" asked Sandra.

"All right. I'll stay if you like," said grandma. "I brought my overnight bag, just in case."

"Mother!" said Billy's mam. "You never told us you were stopping!"

"I didn't think I had to, Alice!" grandma said with a sniff. "I'm not a child, you know!" She wiped her nose on a hanky she took from the sleeve of her new dress that she'd bought at the Oxfam shop for 50 pence. Then she said, "I've left my bag in the back of the van, Steven, if you'd just like to get it out for me?"

CHAPTER EIGHT

A New Life

SOON IT WOULD be Christmas. And if they were lucky, three or four days of sledging and snowfights. But apart from that, the winter was long and dark and depressing. And Billy's dad had told him that this winter would be a particularly bad one.

Billy was preparing the hen-meal in the back-kitchen. His dad was in the other room, in his chair by the fire, enjoying the warmth. He'd just come in from work. It was just like the old days. Only better. His dad didn't work shifts now. Every night he was home in time for the news at five-forty.

Billy's mam was peeling vegetables for a stew, using the new-fangled peeler.

Billy passed her to get the kettle from

NEW

the stove. They always heated the mash when the weather turned nasty. Billy's mother used to say that the hens liked something warm in their bellies on a cold winter night.

"You're a proper expert with that peeler now, Mam," Billy said.

"Practice makes perfect, Billy."

He poured the steaming hot water on to the mash. "You're still not as good as that market man, though."

"I doubt I ever shall be, Billy," she said. "But I'm coming on, and at least it's a change. And there's a lot to be said for a change, pet."

By the time Billy had fed and watered the hens it was dark. They needed no shooing back into their hut when they'd finished. They seemed to want to go to bed early: there was no *Bionic Woman* for them to watch on Friday nights!

Down in the valley the street lamps

were on and the cars were using their sidelights.

But there were no lights on the colliery now. A year ago it would have been lit up like Blackpool Illuminations. But there was hardly anything left of the pit-head, and the pit heap was being slowly flattened. Every day three J.C.B's crawled over it, their noise filling the valley as

they altered the skyline. What would the pit heap be like next summer? Billy wondered. Would there really be flocks of sheep grazing on it? Herds of cows?

Billy's dad was fastening up the pigeons. Dot was over there with him. Billy could hear her tail swishing. She was so pleased just to be with him.

"Dad? You know your new job?"

"What about it, son?"

"Is it better than the pit?"

"Better than the pit?" He laughed. He didn't speak again until he had finished and had come over to where Billy was. "A thousand times better, Billy. It's like a new lease of life for me. You know what I sometimes do? Sometimes, when I'm right on the top of them moors, I just stop the van and I get out and I take a big breath of air, and I think what a lucky man I really am. It's like wine up there. It's champion."

Billy smiled to himself.

"Maybe you *can* teach an old dog new tricks after all, then, Dad?"

He meant his dad when he said that, of course. But his dad misunderstood.

"How do you mean, Billy?" he said, looking round for Dot and slapping his thigh. "Here, Dot! Good girl."

Dot came bounding up to him out of

the darkness. His father bent down to pat her.

"You might be right, Billy. She's getting better. No doubt about that. Tell you what we'll do. Tomorrow's Saturday. We'll take her down to the field, shall we? See if we can get a bit of sense in her?"

Billy couldn't say a word. He was too pleased to speak.

Dot followed his father to the gate, her tail swishing. Just as she went out she knocked something over. A plant pot, perhaps? Or was it one of the pieces of glass that was always leaning against the end of the cold-frame? It didn't matter anyhow. His dad said nothing. He might not even have noticed.

Suddenly Billy felt glad. Perhaps this winter would not be so bad after all.

He discovered he was humming to himself as he locked the allotment gate and started down the steep path after Dot and his father.